Parallax

SINÉAD MORRISSEY was born in 1972 and grew up in Belfast. She is the author of four previous poetry collections. Her awards include the Patrick Kavanagh Award, the Irish Times/Poetry Now Award, first prize in the UK National Poetry Competition and a Lannan Literary Fellowship. Her most recent collection, *Through the Square Window*, was shortlisted for both the T.S. Eliot Prize and the Forward Prize for Best Collection and was a Poetry Book Society Choice. She lectures in creative writing at the Seamus Heaney Centre for Poetry, Queen's University, Belfast.

Also by Sinéad Morrissey from Carcanet Press

There Was Fire in Vancouver
Between Here and There
The State of the Prisons
Through the Square Window

SINÉAD MORRISSEY

Parallax

CARCANET

First published in Great Britain in 2013 by
Carcanet Press Limited
Alliance House
Cross Street
Manchester M2 7AQ

www.carcanet.co.uk

A CIP catalogue record for this book is available from the British Library.

ISBN 978 1 84777 204 6

The publisher acknowledges financial assistance from Arts Council England

Typeset by XL Publishing Services, Exmouth
Printed and bound in England by SRP Ltd, Exeter

for Sofia

Acknowledgements

Thanks are due to the editors of the following publications in which some of these poems, or versions of them, have previously appeared: *The Antioch Review*, *Archipelago*, *The Atlanta Review*, *The Cincinnati Review*, *The Edinburgh Review*, *English Studies: A Journal of English Literature and Language*, *The Irish Pages*, *Jubilee Lines* (Faber and Faber, 2012), *The Moth*, *New Walk*, *PN Review*, *Poetry Daily*, *Poetry Ireland Review*, *Poetry London*, *Poetry Review*, *The SHOp*, *Southword*, *The Stinging Fly*, *Tongue: A Journal of Literature of Art* and *The Yellow Nib*.

'1801', 'Puzzle', '"Ladies in Spring" by Eudora Welty', 'Lighthouse', 'A Matter of Life and Death', 'Photographs of Belfast by Alexander Robert Hogg', 'Fool's Gold', 'Last Winter' and 'Blog' were recorded for the Poetry Archive.

Thanks are due to the Arts Council of Northern Ireland and the National Lottery for a Major Artist Individual Award in 2012.

Contents

1801	11
Baltimore	12
Shadows	13
Shostakovich	14
Photographs of Belfast by Alexander Robert Hogg	15
Home Birth	18
A Day's Blindness	19
Display	21
Fur	23
Fool's Gold	24
Jigsaw	26
Puzzle	27
Photographing Lowry's House	28
Migraine	32
Daughter	33
V is for Veteran	38
Last Winter	40
A Matter of Life and Death	41
Signatures	44
Through the Eye of a Needle	45
The Doctors	46
The Evil Key	48
Yard Poem	50
Lighthouse	51
The Coal Jetty	52
'Ladies in Spring' by Eudora Welty	54
The Mutoscope	56
The House of Osiris in the Field of Reeds	57
The Party Bazaar	59
The High Window	61
Peacocks and Butterflies	63
A Lie	66
Blog	67
Notes	69

PARALLAX: (*Astron.*) Apparent displacement, or difference in the apparent position, of an object, caused by actual change (or difference) of position of the point of observation; *spec.* the angular amount of such displacement or difference of position, being the angle contained between the two straight lines drawn to the object from the two different points of view, and constituting a measure of the distance of the object.

—*Oxford English Dictionary*

1801

A beautiful cloudless morning. My toothache better.
William at work on The Pedlar. Miss Gell
left a basket of excellent lettuces; I shelled
our scarlet beans. Walked out after dinner for letters—
met a man who had once been a Captain begging for alms.

★

The afternoon airy & warm. No letters. Came home
via the lake, which was near-turquoise
& startled by summer geese.
The soles on this year's boots are getting worn.
Heard a tiny wounded yellow bird, sounding its alarm.

★

William as pale as a basin, exhausted with altering…
I boiled up pears with cloves.
Such visited evenings are sharp with love
I almost said *dear, look.* Either moonlight on Grasmere
                              —like herrings!—
or the new moon holding the old moon in its arms.

Baltimore

In other noises, I hear my children crying—
in older children playing on the street
past bedtime, their voices buoyant
in the staggered light; or in the baby
next door, wakeful and petulant
through too-thin walls; or in the constant
freakish pitch of Westside Baltimore
on *The Wire*, its sirens and rapid gunfire,
its beleaguered cops haranguing kids
as young as six for propping up
the dealers on the corners, their swagger
and spitfire speech; or in the white space
between radio stations when no voice
comes at all and the crackling static
might be swallowing whole a child's
small call for help; even in silence itself,
its material loops and folds enveloping
a ghost cry, one I've made up, but heard,
that has me climbing the stairs, pausing
in the hall, listening, listening hard,
to—at most—rhythmical breathing
but more often than not to nothing, the air
of the landing thick with something missed,
dust motes, the overhang of blankets, a ship
on the Lough through the window, infant sleep.

Shadows

My shadow this morning on the station platform
looks impossibly stretched and beaten thin:
a stiltwalker's shadow, all legs and no torso;
a dun metal casing left after a hammering.

Late February sunlight, winter's filigree
still inside it. Beside me the bins
are casting vast apparitions
of themselves over the yellow line

while my head has lain itself down
across the tracks, the way it wanted to
all those years ago, in Amsterdam,
near the *Leidesplein*, before the see-through

boy with his quiver of arrows
could claim me as his own.
It jolts bolt upright as the Carrickfergus train
vanishes in the opposite direction.

I could be a dissident in a textbook in Soviet Russia
discovered after the print run
and painstakingly blackened out by each teacher,
or a stage set after the lights have blown

on a tinkly Victorian performance in reds and golds.
I could be blood in a black-and-white video.
The platform is shining with salt.
My shadow displaced at the waist is taking a bow.

Lady other, Lady mine, if I stood here all morning
I'd watch you retracting back like drowning soap.
Shadows of candles on church walls at Evensong
manifest not as flame, but smoke.

Shostakovich

The wind and its instruments were my secret teachers.
In Podolskaya Street I played piano for my mother
—note for note without a music sheet—while the wind
in the draughty flat kept up: tapping its fattened hand
against the glass, moaning through the stove, banging
a door repeatedly out on the landing—
the ghost in the machine of Beethoven's *Two Preludes*
Through All the Major Keys, that said they lied.

Later I stood in a wheat field and heard the wind make music
from everything it touched. The top notes were the husks:
fractious but nervous, giddy, little-voiced,
while underneath a strong strange melody pulsed
as though the grain was rigging, or a forest.

In all my praise and plainsong I wrote down
the sound of a man's boots from behind the mountain.

Photographs of Belfast by Alexander Robert Hogg

The year the Great Ship Herself
is fitted out
at the mouth of the Lagan,

her panelling
drilled through and threaded
with miles of electric cables

and her gymnasium
horses finally bolted
down—

fifty cubic tonnes
of soot
falls over the city

in drifts, in rain, in air
breathed out then in again,
re-textured as dust.

He notices
the stark potential
of tarnished water

for the glass-plate photograph:
how there are slate tones
and oiliness together

and how, in standing pools
and running drains,
it coats the children's feet

with ubiquitous, gritty ink.
Alleyways and back yards
snag on his mind:

he can barely pass an entry
without assessing
the effect the diagonal

of a porterhouse roof
beside a streetlight
might produce, whereas

to photograph a yard
on Little York Street—
its ruin of toppled bricks

and broken guttering,
the windows of its houses,
open holes—

is to cast the viewer out
onto the no-man's-land
of her own estate

and to prove the eye is banked
as much by what unravels
as by flint.

There is the tidy shop
he makes his tidy living in
selling a wallet

of possible poses
for posterity: the Father
with his watch-chain,

the Sailor on his stool.
But for this commission
from the Corporation

he's sending home
dispatches from Sebastopol
Street in which

a man by the railings
ghosts himself
by turning his head too soon.

One cannot tell
if the room in the photograph
entitled *Number 36*

is inhabited—
light from the missing
upper storey is shafted

by jutting planks,
the fire-black walls
are crystalline

and yet outside similar terraces
with crumbling masonry
and dark for doors,

in bedraggled
unspeakable arcs
he's conjured with his shillings,

each child strong enough
to manage it
carries a child.

Home Birth

The night your sister was born in the living-room
you lay on your bed, upstairs, unwaking,
Cryptosporidium frothing and flourishing
through the ransacked terraces of your small intestine
so that, come morning, you, your bedding, me,
the midwife even, had to be stripped and washed.
Your father lifted you up like a torch
and carried you off to the hospital.

You came back days later, pale and feverish,
and visited us in the bedroom in your father's arms.
You turned your head to take her in: this black-haired,
tiny, yellow person who'd happened while you slept.
And you were the white dot of the television, vanishing—
vanishing—just before the screen goes dark.

A Day's Blindness

December. The year at the back of it
blown and shrunk to dark
in the morning, dark in the afternoon
and the light in between
like the pale blue flicker of a pilot light
in a boiler's black intestine.

There was the usual breakfast
—coffee, soda bread, jam—
neither one of them speaking.
Her slept-on hair. The papers
still to go out for and a walk
to the top of the road and back,

past crows' nests fisted in trees,
to look at the Lough. It happened
at once: no jolt, no warning,
no shutter cranking low
over everything, no shadows
starting off on the periphery

like hares in fields
then gradually thickening.
He stood up to carry his plate and cup
to the sink and couldn't see.
He sat back down. The clocks
went on consuming Saturday.

He would have needed practice
at being blind to pretend to be sighted.
He had none, so she saw.
The son was away in Florida.
He asked her to leave, and for hours then,
as through the womb's wall,

he heard her about the house,
moving around upstairs,
using the bathroom, and perhaps
just once—or twice?—
saying something soft
and incoherent into the telephone.

Outside, at a quarter to four,
a watery sunset broke over
the squat hills. He couldn't tell
the lifting and the thud
of the returning dark apart.
He sat on at the table,

rolling crumbs beneath his thumbs
and waiting, either for what was taken
to be handed back—
the fridge, the kettle, his cuff-linked shirt—
or for the kleptomaniac visitor
he couldn't lock out

to be done with it, finally,
to sever the link—
to haul him up out of his chair,
into the hall, and through the brown door
to a garden ruined with hooves
and there would be

horses set loose from the Bond Yard
where his father worked
in the Hungry Thirties,
their coats engrained with soot
and their heads encased in steam,
accusing him.

Display

movement is life
—slogan of the Women's League of Health and Beauty, 1930–1939

Hyde Park, 1936. Cold enough for scarves and hats
among the general populace, but not for the fifteen thousand women
from the League of Health and Beauty performing callisthenics
on the grass. It could be snowing, and they of Bromley-Croydon,
Slough,
Glasgow, Belfast, would don no more than a pair of satin knickers
and a sleeveless satin vest to spin and stretch and bow
the body beautiful. Athens in London, under a sodden sky,
and Winnie and Molly and Doris metamorphosed.

On the edge of the revolving staves of arms and legs,
pale as comfrey—an army not yet on the move but almost ready—
there are tents for scones and tea. Kiddies, brought to watch
in caps and plaits, wriggle on deckchairs. Their mothers
carry vast, forbidden handbags on their laps and smell
of Lily of the Valley. All around the periphery,
in huddled clumps of overcoats and smoke,
from offices and railway yards, men joke and talk, gesticulate—

but mostly they just look, quietly and sharply focused,
like eyeing up the horses at a racecourse, but with much more choice.
For those crammed in steaming picturehouses later, a commentator,
brusquely charmed, declares *the perfection of British womanhood:
to them belongs the future!*—while the ghost of Mary Bagot Stack,
whose dream this is, smiles back. Their hair cut short, slim,
co-ordinated as the League of German Maidens or a chorus set
from Hollywood, fit for birth, the women twirl and kick,

do foot-swings and scissor-jacks, link hands or fall
suddenly flat as pegs in a collapsible building, then bounce back
up again, for movement is life and they are keeping moving.
To hell with it, they may as well be saying. Twist.
To hell with Lizzie Evans and her bitching hate.
With blood and vinegar. With getting in the tin bath last.
With laddered stockings. With sore wrists at the factory.
I've got the fresh-air-body they promised me. Twist. Its electricity.

Fur

At 25 and 29 respectively, Hans Holbein's
burly furred ambassadors haven't got long to go:
the pox, the plague, the ague, a splinter
in the finger, a scratch at the back of the throat
or an infection set into the shoulder joint
might carry them off, in a matter of writhing
hours, at any instant—

                Too obvious a touch

to set the white skull straight.   Better
to paint it as something other: driftwood
up-ended by magic from the right-hand side
of the tesserae carpet; to let it hang
like an improbable boomerang just under
the clutch of pipes, the lute with the broken
string, still casting a shadow…

For there is bewitchery in those brown beards yet—
in the (slightly) rakish tilt to the saucer hat
of the ambassador on the left.

Fool's Gold

For other men
the world is a woman
and their craving assuageable.
To say *every waking thought*
is surely to exaggerate,
but in my bowel

as much as in
my brain, my foremost sin
is gold. Its pristine glint and heft,
vaulted beneath my palace
in coins and necklaces,
masks, goblets,

was not enough
to stop the famished wolf
of my desire, to shut its throat.
So therefore, John Wright,
who stole and dipped
in your magic vat

a rose from my
buttonhole, smilingly,
and then lifted it out transmuted
into gold—you proffered
the key and did
not know it

to a blissful
plenitude, my soul's
ultimate, jubilant relief. I witnessed
tarnished candelabras
lowered as brass
come up licked

by the sun;
your workshop hung
with busts and angels, merchants' seals
and swords so luminescent
light itself sent
spies to steal

their secret.
And while chariots
and stallions and my own slick
mounted, radiant self bloomed
instantly in my mind,
I knew the trick

to set me there,
my newfound noble elixir,
the needle to be passed through,
the famed alchemical ingot
I could not do without—
was you.

Jigsaw

The Royal children have been sent a gift—
A map of Europe from 1766
Complete with longitude, painted onto wood,
Like any other map in brown and green and red,
But then disfigured: cut up into parts,
A disassembly of tiny courts
Strewn across the table. There is a key
To help the children slot, country by country,
The known traversable world in place:
Little Tartary, Swedish Lapland, France,
The Government of Archangel. The sea
Has been divided into squares, crudely,
As though the cast-iron sides of nations
Still applied (but with more attention
To geometry) while the engraver's signature
—A circle, his name, a folded flower—
Has been deftly sawn in half. If successful,
The three young princes and the oldest girl
(This is not, after all, a lesson in diplomacy
So she can play too) will, ironically,
Undo the puzzle's title and its claim:
Europe Divided in its Kingdoms
Shall be Europe reconfigured, whole.
They start in the top left corner with the scale
Then fill the other corners in: 'Part of Africa',
A scroll, the blank of simply 'Asia'
Rolling off to hordes and steppes and snow
Beyond the boundary. Outlines follow,
Aided by exquisite lettering:
'The Frozen Ocean' solidifies across the map's ceiling...
And so the Royal children spend an hour
Staring and exclaiming, clicking together
(What joy!) the angled buttress of a continent—
Their own unlikely island on a slant
By its farthest edge, and in their trance ignore
What will no longer fit: Aortearoa, America.

Puzzle

for Sheila Llewellyn

Vitya pledges his brigade of Pioneers will plant
half as many fruit trees as the other Pioneers.
Kiryusha pledges *his* brigade, the best of the detachment,
will match the trees of all brigades together, including Vitya's.
Their brigades work the last shift simultaneously.
The preceding brigades of the detachment
plant forty trees. Both pledges are fulfilled exactly.
How many trees does the whole detachment plant?

Answer: a kind of Latin, finished and intricate,
or a box of glass-plate negatives from 1887
unearthed by accident of Newcastle cloth market.
The Oceanic Whitetip Shark. Ectoplasm.
Natasha Ivanova on her collective farm
working out the most efficient way to harvest cotton.

Photographing Lowry's House

And then he died.
And so I drove to where
he'd lived. I don't know why.
To stand across the street,
perhaps, hands in my pockets,
a happenstance observer

of the bricks, the Georgian
front, the chimney pots
and guttering, the bin,
the hedge, the fence,
appearing all-at-once
untenanted, bereft—

to take a photograph
or two of how that looked.
But his house was a smashed
hive, all industry and ruin:
the door was open;
vans with their backs

thrown wide cluttered
the driveway; men he never knew
in life were loading up
painting after painting—
portraits, landscapes, mill-scenes—
stripping every room

of his obsessions.
And so I intervened, crying theft
and history, and they listened.
And I was given half
an hour to photograph
what was left

before they finished.
Light inside the hallway,
even in February: without a flash
the staircase seeming flounced
in the train of a bridal dress,
shimmery

as the white space
in the foreyards of the factories
his buckled, blank-faced
people bent their bodies to.
The mantelpiece in the living-room
strewn with stories—

postcards, knick-knacks,
impromptu napkin sketches;
the bar-talk of the clocks,
each set to a different time
in case their simultaneous chimes
distressed him; likenesses

of his parents scowling down.
But as though I stood in Lascaux
among its sprinting fawns
and my very breath
was wrecking what I stared at,
there were absences also:

squares of thin-lined stains
where, moments earlier,
pictures in their frames
had kept their residence—
impossible now to distinguish
which. My camera

clicked and whirled.
Upstairs I found his studio.
I changed the film.
They'd been in here
but not for long—everywhere,
archipelagos

of canvases he'd lain
against the window or the walls
still held their chains.
Persons, closer up than anything
of his I'd ever seen:
a boy and girl,

huddled and lovely
against a fogged-out background;
a man and his family,
everyone in it
round-shouldered and perplexed
by being found;

a child hitching a lift
in a barrow. And then the sea,
over and over: with a black ship
smoking into harbour,
or a distraction of yachts, or
waves and horizon only—

de-peopled, the tide
that one day didn't turn
but swallowed
the cacophony
of Salford and Pendlebury
and kept on coming on.

I had a minute
in the bedroom with Rossetti's
luscious women, standing silent
guard about his bed.
The counterpane re-made.
And then the foreman called me

from the first-floor landing—
they had to be getting on,
I should be going—and I had time
for a final shot
on my botched way out:
his trilby and his mac, hanging

from a hook, in black and white.

Migraine

And it's happening yet again:
vandals set loose in the tapestry room
with pin-sharp knives. Such lovely scenes
as this day's scrubbed-white clouds
and shock of scarlet blooms
across the wasteground

looking abruptly damaged—
stabbed-though from the back
so that a dozen shining pin-sized
holes appear at random. Then widen.
Soon even the grass has been unpicked,
the gorse hacked open.

I can no longer see your face.
Posed in unravelling sleeves
and disappearing lace,
I have given up all hope for what was whole—
the monkey under the orange tree,
the tatterdemalion nightingale.

Daughter

after Robert Pinsky

I

She wakes at 7am—
her internal clock
unstintingly accurate—
and can sleep twelve hours
at a stretch without
losing hold of her last thought.
The grievance she fell
asleep with: *you didn't*
get me rice milk or
you didn't sing me
song 'bout Tommy Thumb—
her dawn declaration.
Though she'll also ask
is it morning?
just to check
she hasn't missed
the best and purest
portion of her day, the bit
with her brother and breakfast
in it, by being away.

II

The dresses and tops
in her wardrobe
smell of fabric conditioner—
sugar, vanilla, baking soda—
and are frequently washed.
The clothes she harries
off and leaves in heaps
on stairs and sofas
so she can flash
about the house
with nothing on—
a moon-pale, decelerating
balloon—recall whiskey:
layered, earthy, consisting
of neither sweat nor
excrement but of what
her deeper body's left
behind itself in warmth.
I cannot tell the strands
of it apart.

III

Cut off by the Atlantic,
half her family
are permanently absent
though she hasn't
noticed this yet.
Her world is still
the roof over 'safe'
in the Japanese pictograph.
Her fiercest, non-human
attachments are to
vibrantly coloured objects
—orange plate, red fork—
she cannot eat without.
She's learning this house
like a psalm: the crack
in the kitchen sink,
the drawers and all
their warring contents,
the geography of each room
immutable as television.

IV

When visitors come
she's keen to show them
the most horrific thing
she knows: Rien Poortvliet's
picture of a Snotgurgle
in the *Bantam Book of Gnomes*.
Scabrous, radically
lopsided, huge—
he's forcing a gnome
through a mangle
while his sidekick-
black rat laughs. The book
falls open at his face.
She might be Persephone,
bravely showing off
what she's survived,
but it's probably the snot
she's more delighted by:
the viscous, glittering rivulets
he hasn't wiped away.

V

In Timothy Leary's
eight-circuit system
of human evolution
there's a drug for every stage.
Acquiring language
or the Symbol State
(concerning itself with maps
and artefacts) is mimicked
by amphetamines:
crystal meth, benzedrine.
Silent too long as an infant,
our daughter talks all day—
her toys, her toes,
her pictures, her minutely
attenuated hierarchy
of friends—
like a businessman
on the last train home
after one too many espressos,
selling you his dream.

V is for Veteran

A soldier returned from a war
was how my P6 spelling book put it: I saw

　　　cripples with tin cans for coins
　　　in dusty scarlet, back from some spat of Empire.

　　　　　　Later I became aware of buildings
　　　　　　built in squares around a courtyard

where every room looked down
to a fountain

　　　rinsing and bleaching the light
　　　assiduously as the women

　　　　　　who in folded hats like wings
　　　　　　washed clean their wounds.

My erstwhile stepfather was one
for whom Vietnam

　　　was a constantly recurring dream—
　　　the jungle inching its tendrils

　　　　　　into his lungs until he becomes
　　　　　　half-man, half-vine, asphyxiating.

The word itself has a click in it.
It halts before the ending.

　　　Boats left stranded in trees.
　　　The ones that survive are amphibian.

　　　　　　As I speak, there is something muscled
　　　　　　and bloody in the sink

the boy young enough to be my son
spat out and I can't look.

     I don't know how he got inside my house.
     The stereo is playing *Buckets of Rain*

         by Dylan,
         over and over again.

Last Winter

was *not like last winter*, we said, when winter
had ground its iron teeth in earnest: Belfast
colder than Moscow and a total lunar eclipse
hanging its Chinese lantern over the solstice.
Last winter we wore jackets into November
and lost our gloves, geraniums persisted,
our new pot-bellied stove sat unlit night
after night and inside our lungs and throats,
embedded in our cells, viruses churned out
relaxed, unkillable replicas of themselves
in the friendlier temperatures. Our son
went under. We'd lie awake, not touching,
and listen to him cough. He couldn't walk
for weakness in the morning. Thoracic,
the passages and hallways in our house
got stopped with what we would not say—
how, on our wedding day, we'd all-at-once
felt shy to be alone together, back
from the cacophony in my tiny, quiet flat
and surrounded by flowers.

A Matter of Life and Death

On the afternoon I'm going into labour so haltingly it's still easy
    to bend and breathe, bend and breathe, each time the erratic clamp
        sets its grip about my pelvis, then releases—

I take a nap, eat lunch and while you pen a letter to our impending
                                                offspring
    explaining who we are, what there is on offer in the house
    we don't yet know we'll leave, to be handed over

on his eighteenth birthday like a key to the demesne, sit front-to-back
    on an upright chair in the living-room and switch on the television.
    World War II. David Niven is faltering after a bombing op

in a shot-up plane. *Conservative by nature, Labour by conviction,*
    he quotes Sir Walter Raleigh: *O give me my scallopshell of quiet,*
        my staff of faith to walk upon, while a terrified American radio girl

listens in. It's all fire and ravenous engine noise—he can't land
    because the fuselage is damaged and he hasn't a parachute.
        Then, because he'd *rather fall than fry,* he bales out anyway—

a blip on the screen vanishing into cloud cover. The girl hides her
                                        face in her hands.
    The baby drops a fraction of an inch and the next contraction hurts.
    I know I'm at the gentlest end of an attenuated scale

of pain relief: climbing the stairs, a bath, two aspirin, tapering down
                                              as the hours
    roll on (and we relocate to hospital) to gas and air, pethidine,
    a needle in the spine, and go out to walk the sunny verges

of our cul-de-sac like a wind-up, fat-man toy, tottering every five
                                          minutes or so
    into a bow. Nobody's home. The bins are still out on the road
    after this morning's pick-up. The light is slant and filled

with running gold. Back inside, the film has switched to Technicolor
    monochrome: an anachronistic afterlife in grey in which dead
                                                                airmen
        sign in under 'name' and 'rank', the Yanks smack gum

and swagger, *isn't this swell?* and a legion of otherworldly women
    with hair rolled high as dunes hand out enormous plaster wings
        to the just-deceased. The dead are invoiced for,

like battleships or teapots, their names on the list ticked off
    as they swing through each allotted doorway clean and whole
        and orderly—the incomprehensible machinery of life and death

a question of books that balance. And there's this sudden tug inside,
    rigging straining taut and singing, and I cry out for the first time,
        and in you come to coax and soothe as though I'm doing
                                                        something—

running a marathon, climbing a mountain—instead of being forced
                                                        back down
    into my seat by some psychopathic schoolmarm over and over again,
        stay. And I think of my granny and her *forty-six hours*

of agony, shifting my mother from one world to the next, and how
                                                        that birth
        cut short her happiness at the Raleigh bicycle factory in Nottingham
            where her youth was spent in *secret war work*, typing up invoices.

Back in heaven, there's about as much commotion as there's been
                                                        in a million
    years (a slight shake of the head by the woman in charge, a sigh)
        because David Niven, who should have arrived but hasn't,

landed on a beach and—how?—survived, met the American radio
                                                        operator
    as she cycled home after the night-shift, and fell in love. He must
                                                        be sent for.
        Down below, they're already looking post-coital: picnicking
                                                        in civvies

on a homespun Tartan rug in a Technicolor rose garden. I'm not
supposed
to show up at the hospital for hours, or not until the cervix
has done its slow, industrial cranking-wide enough to be marked

by a thumb-span, and the problem is I don't know what that
means, or how to tell,
or how much worse the pain is going to get (answer: a lot)
and so the afternoon grows hot and narrow and you abandon

your confessions altogether and the botched clock of paradise with
seven hands
across its face ticks on the wall. *I've seen it many times,* said my granny,
when a new life comes into a family, an old life goes out—

as though there were checks and balances, birth weighted against death
like a tidy invoice, and a precise amount of room allotted the
living.
Before we inch upstairs to the bathroom to test what sweet
relief

is granted, after all, by a bath and lavender oil, I catch sight of a
magical marble escalator—the original stairway to heaven—with
David Niven
captive on its steps being hauled away to the sound of a
clanking bell

from his radiant girlfriend, and I imagine my granny, who died
three weeks ago
on a hospital ward in Chesterfield, *making room* as she herself
predicted,
not dumb and stricken and hollowed out with cancer

but young, glamorous, childless, free, in her 1940s' shoes and sticky
lipstick,
clicking about the office of new arrivals as though she owns it,
flicking open the leather-bound ledger and asking him to sign.

Signatures

Belfaste is a place meet for a corporate town, armed with all commodities,
as a principal haven, wood and good ground, standing also upon a border...
—extract from a letter to the Privy Council from the Earl of Essex, 1573

I

Where nothing was, then something. Six months ago
most of this was sludge and a gangrenous slip-way
dipping its ruined foot in the sea—a single rusted gantry
marking the spot where a small town's population
of Protestant men built a ship the size of the Empire State Building.
Smashed cars and wreckers' yards flourished in between.

II

A skin-stripping wind. This morning I walk on concrete
smooth as a runway with a full-scale outline laid in light
of the uppermost deck. Railings as over a stern.
Grass. Seating. The memorial for the dead hosts names
I can't pronounce—*Sjöstedt, Taussig, Backström*—
in immaculate glass. Once, I count a surname seven times.

Through the Eye of a Needle

Still shorter than my hip
but solid, heavy as a scooped-full
coal-scuttle, hair so fingerwrapped and knotted
it stands in coils about her ears and won't comb flat,
cherubic, with that dimpled roll of fat above the buttocks
the stubby painted angels carry brightly, her feet and hands a fan
she opens frequently to admire the slotted hinges of her bones,
to blow between the gaps, arm-skin like powder down,
an almost-constant frown atop a round bright box
with treasure in it: seamless lips, even teeth,
eyes that loop the swallows up

on their traceable tethers
to harry them, upside-down, into
the huge room of her brain and make them fit
the vivid, random furniture pre-assembled there—
buttercup petals crushed on her palm, the Teapot Song,
dust motes and the taste of rust, shadows under her cot that grow
vast without a night-light, hunger, always satisfied,
its own fat child in a caul and sleepiness a wall
you dig-a-hole-and-curl-up under—
where they leave their threaded
flight-path like the imprint
on a carpet of a stain.

The Doctors

blurted it out like a Polaroid
                              —Paul Muldoon

In this country
they are desecrating photographs—
those that tell the truth of their own flown moment
simply as it was, that are naïve as schoolchildren
set down in a bewildering classroom and bid to speak
their name and place of birth in a foreign tongue,
who revert, instinctively, to their own, as slates
and straps and canes rain down upon them.

It is the camera's
inherent generosity of outlook
which is more often than not at fault:
the one-whose-name-we-dare-not-whisper
sitting at breakfast with Our Great Leader
on holiday in the Urals, or idly grinding his teeth
in a dim committee room, his glasses like miniature
headlights reflecting the flash.

With scissors,
nail files, ink and sellotape, he has been vanished—
alongside other party operatives who touched
His sleeve, or didn't clap for long enough, or loved
their wives, or laughed, or who pointed the way
down some rickety steps as though He needed help
—whole politburos cropped to a man, or at most
a handful of survivors ranged around a chess table,

scratched absences
over their shoulders made luminous as moons.
It is addictive: the urge to utter a language
both singular and clean. It is progressive—
how the power to transform a conspirator into a pillar
transmutes, in turn, to the eradication
of the accidental as a class of photograph:
how litter, bleak weather, a sneer,

or too many smiling
parents who later disappeared are also doctored.
And should anyone be missed—turning up
in textbooks before the grave extent
of their transgression's been established—
a nation's girls and boys, all trained
in proper parlance, their fingers stained with soot,
draw over women's faces black balloons.

The Evil Key

In woods and lakes, car boots, freezers, huts,
in ministers' apartments where their flailing last

went on too long, garrotted, poisoned, hanged
or sliced in half and lain like Solomon's child

on the bridge of a border between two countries—
the myriad murdered dead of Scandinavia

are seeping their slow corrosion into the air, into
the tap water, and must be found. So many crimes

unsolved you'd think those dressed-down cops
in their open-plan offices balanced books

on their heads all day or practised on the sly
for the Eurovision Song Contest. But wait—

Denmark and Sweden's cleverest women
are on their way: obsessed, lonely, semi-autistic

and wired as no man with them ever is
to sense, without exactly evidence, where corpses

have been left: plastered into a crevice in a flat
in an affluent suburb or strung amongst the cables

of a lift-shaft in a disused meat-packing plant.
F# Minor, writes Johann Mattheson in 1713,

is *abandoned, singular, misanthropic,* and *leads
to great distress. We cannot well accompany*

the Devil in any other key. It will invert anything—
Jingle Bells, Home on the Range, Dick Van Dyke's

Chim Chim Cheree—turning them hopeless
and ironic, just as glass-walled houses

in the forest, immaculate kitchens, flat-pack rooms
sprung wide and nifty public transport systems

translate to mist in the brightly lit underground
hall of the coroner's workspace where three

blonde girls from the badminton squad
have hit their brutal terminus. We are given

less than a second
with their lacerated legs and hands.

Then cut to the churning sea with the moon on it—
the music making it worse—then nothing.

Yard Poem

for Paul Maddern

The rat on your salvaged pallet out the back
among pots, bricks, paperweights,
bees made of glass, a litter
of pink petals from the balsawood trellis,
the blown-open tongues of the honeysuckle—
is already a nest for flies and getting rained on.
It shifts its weight every fifteen minutes or so
so we know it's still living.

With bodies as blue as a peacock's waistcoat
or coal's first concession to fire,
the flies shimmer at intervals
along the animal's flank: so still
you'd think they'd died together.
Now neither sex, nor leaf-sweep, nor thunder
can cleave them. The eyes of the rat are sealed tight
as though pencilled shut with eyeliner.

More flies alight. It rains harder. I can't look.
The rat draws its consciousness
back into its own scuttled bone-shack.
And the blue of the flies shines, jewelled,
unfazable, a mineral attack
on the walls of our final kingdom—
burglars, with a sense of grievance,
desecrating the Hall of Ishtar.

Lighthouse

My son's awake at ten, stretched out along
his bunk beneath the ceiling, wired and watchful.
The end of August. Already the high-flung
daylight sky of our Northern solstice dulls
earlier and earlier to a clouded bowl;
his Star of David lamp and plastic moon
have turned the dusk to dark outside his room.

Across the Lough, where ferries venture blithely
and once a cruise ship, massive as a palace,
inched its brilliant decks to open sea—
a lighthouse starts its own nightlong address
in fractured signalling; it blinks and bats
the swingball of its beam, then stands to catch,
then hurls it out again beyond its parallax.

He counts each creamy loop inside his head,
each well-black interval, and thinks it just for him—
this gesture from a world that can't be entered:
the two of them partly curtained, partly seen,
upheld in a sort of boy-talk conversation
no one else can hear. That private place, it answers,
with birds and slatted windows—I've been there.

The Coal Jetty

Twice a day,
  whether I'm lucky enough
    to catch it or not,

the sea slides out
  as far as it can go
    and the shore coughs up

its crockery: rocks,
  mussel banks, beach glass,
    the horizontal chimney stacks

of sewer pipes,
  crab shells, bike spokes.
    As though a floating house

fell out of the clouds
  as it passed
    the city limits,

Belfast bricks, the kind
  that also built the factories
    and the gasworks,

litter the beach.
  Most of the landing jetty
    for coal's been washed

away by storms; what stands—
  a section of platform
    with sky on either side—

is home now to guillemots
  and cormorants
    who call up

the ghosts of nineteenth-
    century hauliers
        with their blackened

beaks and wings.
    At the lowest ebb,
        even the scum at the rim

of the waves
    can't reach it.
        We've been down here

before, after dinner,
    picking our way
        over mudflats and jellyfish

to the five spiked
    hallways underneath,
        spanned like a viaduct.

There's the stink
    of rust and salt,
        of cooped-up

water just released
    to its wider element.
        What's left is dark and quiet—

barnacles, bladderwrack,
    brick—but book-ended
        by light,

as when Dorothy
    opens her dull
        cabin door

and what happens outside is Technicolor.

'Ladies in Spring' by Eudora Welty

a translation

Dewey is going fishing with his father to the swamp.
The earth is powder-dry. The sky is laden.
The river's a half-drained basin with the bottom poking through:
mud, tree-stumps, driftwood spiked like antlers, rocks.
They have a pole each slung over one shoulder
and a bucket for the catch. There are no fish.

Miss Hattie Purcell from the post office is making it rain.
She surprises them, sitting in the puddle of her clothes,
concentrating. Of everyone back at the Royals—
the schoolmaster, the Seed & Feed owner—
only she has the power. They go round her
like skirting a preacher they haven't the time for.

The indigo bushes are latticed with climbing vines.
Violets are blooming, and frowsy white flowers
Dewey doesn't know the name of that happen in spring.
They run a rickety plank to a smashed-up bridge
in the middle of the Little Muscadine
and drop their bated lines. Schtum as a heron,

Miss Hattie sits rigid on the crest of the riverbank,
whatever language magic might be made of
running in her mind. *Blackie!* Then again, *Blackie!*
And here comes his father's name, shot across
to them out of the maples. *Blackie!* Miss Hattie
doesn't move. Some other lady entirely

has gone and placed her round bright face in the branches
where a circle of sun has landed and uttered this cry.
Then she runs away. The swamp is still as a Sunday.
She must be about to die, thinks Dewey,
watching for his fish. His father flourishes
a lunch from his overall pockets and they laugh.

It starts to rain—yes, praise to heaven rising
where it falls O hallelujahs—one plopped drop at a time.
Soon the river's so ploughed and puckered
it looks like a muddy field you'd step onto and be safe.
And if the rain could be translated into words
Little You and Little Me, Little You and Little Me

would be the closest thing to meaning you could catch.

The Mutoscope

Double Trouble, The Ghost Café, Late at Night
in the Bedroom: each Mutoscope tells its story
to whoever steps right up, drops a penny in its slot

and cranks the handle. Mimicking decency,
the poster shows a solid Victorian gentlewoman
stooping to its glass as though sniffing narcissi

in a window box, her hat a fountain.
A World of Moving Pictures, Very Popular
in Public Places, it is, in fact, an intimate machine

whose jittery flickerings of marital war,
a monkey on a bicycle, or a lady being undressed
from a through-the-keyhole, what-the-butler-saw

perspective, no one else can watch
at the same time. Sir or Madam, yours is the hand
that squares the frame, undoes the catch

at the top of the reel and sets eight hundred
separate photographs tumbling into blackness
against a brown-paper background

but showing you each shot before they vanish.
Only for you do the two mute girls on stage
who falter at first, erratic as static

in the synaptic gap between each image,
imperceptibly jolt to life—
grinning, tap-dancing, morphing into footage,

their arms like immaculate pistons, their legs like knives…
It lasts a minute, their having-been-written onto light.

The House of Osiris in the Field of Reeds

I'm turning forty. Not on my birthday
(still, as I write, six weeks away) but over months.
It's like a migraine: that sludgy disconnectedness
starting in the brain, hours before the hammering.
I've forgotten my name and my husband's name
in the run-up to the full-scale meltdown.

All through last winter, each day
made to bear the pressure of impending loss.
Soon it will no longer be like this. The lean girls
picnicking in the park, their haul of charity-shop
dresses at their feet, listening to the Smiths,
have long since picked themselves up and vanished

down the tall-grass corridor of rooks and smoke.
I can no longer remember their faces, or what
the sky over Dublin inscribed on my skin
the year I'd just left home, or even the impact
of first-time, proper sex, of being unwrapped.
But turning forty banishes my younger self

to a separate outhouse, somewhere stony
and impassable, hot, fly-infested, like the city
of Tetu on the Nile which became the Otherworld
for all of Egypt, and I cannot get across.
Death was so much closer then, of course—
I'd be dead already or at least a grandmother;

if rich, I'd have my orders pre-prepared
for the sarcophagus maker, the Shabti carver,
the weaver of the shroud; I'd have selected
the spells for my coffin-lid, the amulets required
to survive the guarded entrances of the afterlife,
the tricky test with hearts and feathers.

*O exiled one, so you may escape the heat
and torpor of that barren place, and pass instead
to the Field of Reeds, and do no work there,
discover by your grave cloths a replica of yourself
in turquoise faience, fashioned with a basket.
Here, it says. I'll do it. Take me.*

The Party Bazaar

Ingrid in her shawl's been here since nine,
burdening the tables on loan
from the church downstairs with Babushka dolls
and caviar, handkerchiefs and wine

from Yugoslavia, Bulgarian perfume.
My brother and I ask for a job
and are handed pink and white posters
of *Peace & Détente* to decorate the room.

It's trickier than we thought
to stick them straight so secretly we give up.
Almost everyone's smoking.
In the background, *Kalinka* on cassette

belted out by the Red Army Choir
wobbles towards its peak. There's tea,
coffee, Irish stew, and a cool display
of anti-Mrs Thatcher paraphernalia—

pens in the shape of nails for her coffin
we'll buy and use in school.
Shop stewards come, and sympathisers
who, once a year, like Christians,

demonstrate their faith, the odd
bewildered lured-in shopper looking for soap,
or socks, but mostly it's just us:
Card Carriers and the Kids Thereof,

filling up the air with fevered talk. By four,
Rosemary Street's ablaze in the solstice dark.
We pack what's left of the wooden trains and vodka
into crates for another year and repair

to the Duke of York, where once
an *actual* Soviet Representative—tall, thin—
in frost-inflected English gave a speech,
and I clutched my lemonade and was convinced.

The High Window

Honey,

You've requested a Raymond Chandler spin-off,
a spoof in style, but from the blonde's perspective:
let's say the secretary in the one about the coin
called a *Brasher Doubloon*, gone missing
from a Pasadena mansion. We're in this thing together:
busier than a PI who never simply talks but utters
wisecracks like a jeweller stringing pearls;
happier too, more stranded in domestic detail,
but, hell, tonight I've drawn the blinds, clicked on
the tasselled lamp, unplugged the telephone,
set out two highballs, and before the children cry
upstairs, pulled you down beside me by your tie.
So I say, it's like this. Some guy walks into the office
with an unlit cigarette, wearing 'unimpressed'
like a drape-cut jacket, and looks her over.
He looks everything over—plants, ashtrays, furniture—
with a languid, expert eye, the type of man who gives
a girl offence by offering advice about her gloves
or hair or make-up uninvited. He knows too much,
about guns and broads and books and chess,
the likelier scenarios, which kinda hurts his soul
and which kinda makes him smooth and cool and powerful.
Our glasses clink. Then you say, a-okay,
but what's with her? And I don't know. Witchery
in the garden room for sure—towering flaxes
pressed against the pane, an alcoholic mistress
and a life so narrow, probably from the outset,
its pathetic little batch of dull effects
could fit inside one suitcase. Which is not her fault.
And you know what? Maybe hair pulled taut
against her head and a simple linen dress
(so weird he notes it twice) is just her choice.
The whiskey seeps its spiced and easy heat
along our spines, the house is oddly quiet,

and I'm suddenly adrift in how the road
to Idle Valley dips and curves towards
its secret: a thousand lighted windows
on the hill, a moon so sharp its shadows
look cut out with an engraving tool,
and Marlowe in his car, escaping the patrol...

Now kiss me.

Peacocks and Butterflies

Dull summer.
A field of standing corn
we can't imagine ever ripening
and a tunnel of trees so thick we half-expect
Narnia at the end of it—
a halter

of flyblown ivy
round every trunk. A bridge
disappearing in lime-green foliage
arches overhead, a blocked road mouths its dark,
and then the car park,
still empty

except for us
and an ostentation
of peacocks, standing to attention
in front of the toilet-block, whose women have vanished.
Their yowling is anguished,
like coitus

without relief,
and bespeaks just such a place
as this, with crumbling walls and trellises
but with gods at its centre, off-white statuary,
visible heat. It automatically
rehearses grief.

A boy who wants
to be king raises his aquamarine
fan. His throat and belly are shining
through the hanging twilight in the middle of the day.
Then, aggrieved, he turns away
as punishment

on our daughter
who has gone and brought
waving hands and shrieking to his court
so thoughtlessly. His underfeathers ripple like gauze
in a waterfall, outlawing
us from colour.

Inside a moss-
covered Nissen hut left over
from the war, the aristocratic owners
of this once-estate have fed, bred, cocooned, released
thirty-eight species
of moth

and butterfly
to hang out their wings
like washing on the heads of jasmine,
split oranges, nectarines, apple-halves, dish-scourers
soaking in honeywater
and on the eyes

of the hip-cocked
Cupid with a fountain at his feet.
She stands a second in diminished light,
her hair burnished and unruly, her mouth ajar, unsure
of the suddenly tropical air
that feels dropped

from heaven
and its fluttering tenants.
The heat pipes whine, fall silent.
The butterflies lift and settle indiscriminately
and could be unbearably heavy
or knock her down

for all she knows,
like her view of the sea
and its encroaching tides as wholly
unpredictable, as able to swallow the length and breadth
of the beach in a single breath.
Then off she goes,

an injured spouse
fixated on escape, unenthralled
by the swallowtails and the admirals,
back through the hanging shredded plastic curtain
that keeps the insects safe, to a garden
with a playhouse

and a climbing-frame,
where all her wishing terminates.
We finish our visit taking tea and cake
in her make-believe kitchen, obeying her commands,
wiping our mouths on our hands,
calling her name.

A Lie

That their days were not like our days,
the different people who lived in sepia—

more buttoned, colder, with slower wheels,
shut off, sunk back in the unwakeable house

for all we call and knock. And even the man
with the box and the flaming torch

who made his servants stand so still
their faces itched can't offer us what it cost

to watch the foreyard being lost
to cream and shadow, the pierced sky

placed in a frame. Irises under the windowsill
were the colour of Ancient Rome.

Blog

I don't have girlfriends but I do have sex
with a different woman about three times a month.
Sometimes more. Sometimes less. I rarely ask.

They'll stop to talk to me in the supermarket
or on the bus. Off-handedly at first.
They're not made-up or drunk. We don't flirt

or analyse it. There's this tiny electrical thrill
gets passed like an egg-yolk slipping
between the cups of its own split shell.

They take me home. It happens. I leave. Simple.
They don't invite me to dinner or text.
It's easy and clean and consensual.

Then it happens again. Loneliness's overblown—
unless I'm just one of the unnaturally blessed.
My good friend Jack told me to write this down.

Notes

'1801' is inspired by Dorothy Wordsworth's *The Grasmere Journal 1800–1803* (Oxford: Oxford University Press, 1991).

In 'Fool's Gold', Prince Albert addresses John Wright, an English surgeon and inventor, in his electroplating workshop in Birmingham in 1840. The poem is inspired by the episode 'Gold' in the series *A History of Art in Three Colours*, written and presented by James Fox, and first broadcast on BBC Four in July 2012.

'Puzzle' is inspired by Boris A. Kordemsky's *The Moscow Puzzles: 359 Mathematical Recreations* (Harmondsworth: Penguin, 1972).

In 'Photographing Lowry's House', I imagine the speaker to be Denis Thorpe, a photographer for the *Guardian*, who took photographs of the interior of L.S. Lowry's house just after the painter had died.

'A Matter of Life and Death' is inspired by the British film of the same title by Michael Powell and Emeric Pressburger, released in the USA as *Stairway to Heaven* (1946).

'The Doctors' is inspired by David King's *The Commissar Vanishes* (Metropolitan Books, 1997)—a study of how photographs were systematically falsified in Soviet-era Russia.